SECRETS TO LOVING AGAIN: Rekindling the Spark and love in your relationship

Debra Harwood

Table of contents

CHAPTER ONE

INTRODUCTION

Love is a beautiful thing and an all encompassing emotion that breeds intimacy, friendship, intellectual compatibility and sexual attraction. A partnership is held together through love because it has a strong biological foundation. The absence of love in a relationship can make a partner feel doubtful and neglected, which can result in disagreements and worries. This is because love is the foundation of a strong link that keeps marriage/relationship for a lifetime.
Love is frequently at the top of almost everyone's list of the characteristics that make a relationship strong. This demonstrates the strength of love and what it can do to support the maintenance of a relationship.

There are countless reasons why love is essential in every relationship. Without love, you wouldn't be able to put up the effort, focus, sacrifice, and patience necessary to create a relationship that will stay. Love frequently serves as the glue holding a marriage together and could strengthen your relationship with your significant other. The kind of love you experience is shaped by a variety of life experiences but if there are unresolved toxic issues in your marriage, the love will also be toxic. Staying in a loveless relationship can affect your health and relationship negatively.

Every relationship will eventually reach a point where the ferocious excitement of "the beginning" wears off and things start to feel a little...boring. It's more depressing when you realize that your brain and body just cannot maintain the adrenaline-fueled butterfly feeling for a lifetime. But losing the spark doesn't mean you're doomed to despair; you can fall in love again. Falling in love or falling back in it is a conscious decision and while neither partner can make everything perfect, you can absolutely do your share to rekindle your relationship.

BENEFITS OF LOVE

The world revolves on love. Studies have revealed that aside from the initial surge experienced when we initially fell heads over heels for someone, the power of love also elevates your mood. The extraordinary power of love has a greater impact than we might anticipate. From strengthening our hearts, lungs, and immune systems to reducing stress and anxiety, improving sex and even lengthening our lives. Being in love in a solid, stable relationship, whether you're married or just in a long-term relationship, can improve your physical, mental, and emotional wellbeing.

There is no end to the significance of love in marriage/relationships. You and your

spouse can't have a strong, fulfilling relationship without love. This demonstrates the strength of love and what it can accomplish to support the upkeep of a relationship.
Love can enrich both marital and personal life in these ways:

- Increases contentment

Nothing compares to the security and comfort that comes from knowing that someone is watching out for you. Love causes the level of the stress hormone cortisol to rise. Cortisol is frequently thought of as a "Stress Hormone," but in the case of falling in love, it doesn't make you feel nervous but instead it causes you to experience butterflies in your stomach, excitement, and the intense passion you experience during the initial stages of a new relationship.

- Keeps the doctor at bay

A spouse may assist in keeping you accountable. Your spouse could make you get outdoors and take a stroll if you're a natural couch potato. If you were single, you probably wouldn't be bugged by your partner/ spouse to see the dermatologist to get that strange mole checked out. Your spouse's insistence on a doctor's appointment could enable early identification of a more severe problem. Our partners may encourage us to take care of ourselves. Even though you may roll your eyes at the time, your partner's nagging could really save your life!

- Fosters respect

Any wholesome connection is built on respect. Love and trust cannot develop in the absence of respect. When you feel appreciated, you are aware that your words, thoughts, and feelings are important. You are more able to be open and confident in your relationship when your partner respects your thoughts and treats you properly.

- Reduces Stress

The hormones dopamine and oxytocin, which give us the sensation of "flying on a cloud," are released when we first fall in love. The presence of a loving spouse, however, continues to have a good impact on our hormone levels after the initial excitement has subsided.

Studies have repeatedly shown that physical contact, often known as nonverbal love, may reduce the body's production of the stress chemicals. If you've ever had a challenging day at work and your spouse gave you a hug to make you feel better, you've probably had this experience.

The good benefits of love on your hormones go beyond just reducing stress in difficult circumstances. Cortisol, a stress hormone, is directly associated with obesity, exhaustion, and a compromised immune system. Long-term couples often have lower cortisol levels than singles do.

CHAPTER TWO

LOSING LOVE AND PASSION

Many couples who lament about the loss of their relationship's "spark" claim that it is the result of "just growing apart" or the development of tedious routines from which they are unable to escape. This frequently happens after the "honeymoon time" has passed, leading couples to wonder whether it is truly worthwhile for them to be together.

According to research, between 30 and 60 percent of married Americans will have an affair at some point during their marriage. Based on that information, I believe it's critical that we investigate what leads people to grow disinterested in their partners and whether there is anything we can do to prevent it.

These are the primary indications you should watch out for if you're concerned that your marriage or relationship is losing its spark:

- Interacting less frequently

Although you may occasionally need some alone time or have busy schedules, spending time with your partner is essential to maintaining a strong relationship. It's not necessary to spend a lot of money and attend expensive dinners. You can express your sentiments and learn more about your partner's thoughts by just sitting down and talking about your day. Take time out for your relationship and treat them to something special if they are significant to you.

- They don't make you feel unique.

Loved-up partners respect one another. Therefore, it's an obvious falling out of love indicator if "you're more focused on what's lacking and defects. The bad begins to outweigh the good, and your differences become more pronounced and clear.

- You are not being truthful

Are you and your partner withholding information from one another? A healthy relationship depends heavily on communication, thus it should be one of your main objectives. You should work on improving your communication if you aren't being honest with your partner about your genuine feelings and ideas, particularly when it comes to unpleasant feelings.

- You're arguing more frequently or harshly now

Do you feel that the majority of your interactions result in disagreements or physical altercations? Disagreements are one thing, but if they eventually escalate into yelling and insults, you have a serious issue on your hands. Set some ground rules before the discussion begins if your arguments are insulting. Don't permit profanity, name-calling, insults, or talking about one another instead of the problem.

- Comparison to others all the time.

A certain indication that your love is fading is when you start comparing your partner to every possibility you might have if you weren't with them." You start to think any relationship may be superior than the one you're in.

- You're putting off dealing with issues.

It's a sign that you don't care about each other enough to try to resolve matters if you've given up trying to solve difficulties. Unresolved disputes might lead you to assume that love is gone when it is merely buried beneath the resentment and tension. You can't build a sturdy house on a bad foundation, and if you don't take the time to address your issues, you shouldn't anticipate having a happy relationship.

- You don't like being with your spouse.

Is spending time with friends and family more enjoyable than spending time with your partner? Instead of anticipating spending time with your partner, do you frequently look forward to seeing your relatives or hanging out with your friends? Spending time with your partner fosters intimacy.

- You imagine living without your partner.

Do you frequently imagine a fulfilling life without your significant other? The emphasis is on joy because it's perfectly reasonable to imagine your life without your lover. However, if you frequently picture a life without your partner and are content with it, you should try to understand where these emotions are coming from.

- You feel lonely

Being lonely is a major sign that your relationship needs work. Do you think your partner isn't paying attention to you or hearing you? Do they never have time for you because they are always too busy? If you're feeling lonely, take it as a warning sign.

- Intimacy on a physical level is extinct.

If you stop wanting to have sex, it can be a sign you're falling out of love. Being in love with someone involves attraction, which leads to physical closeness. We want sex when we are in good physical condition, attracted to one another, and in love. To the contrary, when we're in good physical health and losing our romantic interest, we cease experiencing arousal and start to feel more amiable, and the sex stops.

- You consider your future plans, but not with them.

Everyone considers their plans for the next month, year, and five years in the future. However, if you often find yourself fantasizing about upcoming trips, moves, or jobs without your significant other in mind, your relationship might not be built for the long haul. In a committed relationship, you are a pair, and the future belongs to the two of you." "There's an issue if someone begins making plans as a 'I' instead of a 'we,'

There is no shame seeking help. It's never pleasant to fall out of love but remember that you are not alone and you can fall in love again.

CHAPTER THREE

REKINDLING LOVE

Love and passion doesn't "fade out."

To keep the fire burning, you carefully arrange the logs, add kindling, and fan the flame. The fire needs constant monitoring and maintenance to prevent it from going out. This is the key to maintaining the love and passion in your relationship.

It's a myth that when we fall out of love, something unforeseen takes place in our relationships to put out a flame that once burned brilliantly. People claim that they "simply don't feel the same way that they once did" about their partner when the intensity of their romantic feelings wanes in a relationship. They frequently assume that their partner is to blame for the loss of passion or have the view that fondness and affection inevitably fade with time. However, according to neuroscience studies, the brain areas linked to early-relationship desire might continue to be active even 20 years into a relationship. Arousal doesn't just fade away.

In actuality, maintaining love in a long-term relationship requires effort, focus, and intention. After the novelty wears off, it's easy to grow accustomed to your partner's presence and develop the habit of taking them for granted. You no longer spend your time thinking about your lover and staring into their eyes; instead, you are consumed with dealing with life's stresses and juggling the demands of job and family. It is normal for new love's obsessional thoughts and compulsive cravings to fade. However, the issue of waning passion appears when you disregard the law of keeping the spark alive: a fire needs to be tended to in order to stay lit.

SECRETS TO REKINDLING LONG LASTING LOVE

It's common to be in a committed relationship, but it's uncommon to be in one that will last a lifetime. Given the diversions in the world we live in today, this is especially true. Regardless of age, the keys to keeping a happy and stable relationship are in the little things. These things can be as straightforward as being punctual, surprising your partner with a small gift, or kissing them good morning every day. Secrets every couple who wishes to have a lasting relationship should be aware of are:

SECRET 1

Listen to your partner always

Genuine listening without "constructing a counter argument in your head" is the cornerstone of effective communication. To become a better listener to your spouse is to truly listen to them so that you may learn from them, not so that you can reply to them.

The best way to show your partner that you care is to listen to them and then show them that you care about how they are feeling by empathizing with their feelings, and providing them with comfort in whatever way they prefer. Failure to respond over time can create a feeling of unimportance which can cause dissatisfaction and distance that stifles a relationship's passion more quickly than the most serious disagreements.

KEYS TO BECOMING AN EFFECTIVE LISTENER

- Stay Focused

How you move, where you gaze, and how you sit or stand shows if you are listening or not. If you want your partner to believe you are paying attention to them, make eye contact, lean forward, engage in comforting facial expressions and avoid distraction. You can reinforce what your partner is saying and improve your ability to concentrate by repeating their words to yourself as they are being said.

- Keep your mouth shut

It's annoying when you keep interrupting your partner when they are speaking. This suggests that you value your opinion over theirs or that you don't have time to listen to them. Never assume that you must speak after a pause or brief period of stillness. It will be simpler for you to comprehend what your partner is trying to say if you let them talk. When the conversation diverts from what they were attempting to tell you about, interruptions that are in response to something they said can also be annoying. In this case, bring up your previous point of discussion.

- It helps a lot to paraphrase.

You may be confident you're hearing "what your partner means for you to hear," by summarizing what your partner is saying. When paraphrasing, you might also add your own version of what was said and ask your companion if that interpretation is accurate. Getting clarification on the issues you're unclear about also demonstrates that you paid attention and are now giving what was stated some thought.

- Avoid making Assumptions by understanding intentions

You want to be certain that you comprehend both what your spouse said and how they feel. Pay close attention to what your partner is saying, and even more so, pay close attention to how they are feeling. If you don't understand, simply ask questions. Also keep in mind that it is okay and even encouraged to express confusion and that you are not being judged. Regardless of whether you concur with their point of view or not, your first responsibility is to get crystal clear about it.

SECRET 2

List the ways that your relationship has improved your life.

Similar to ice cream, relationships may be both addicting and delicious at first, but gradually lose their allure. This is due to the fact that when something positive becomes routine, it is often taken for granted.

In order to combat this, spend 15 minutes writing down all the ways in which your life has been improved by this individual." Include both little accomplishments, such as "He washed the dishes last night," and more significant ones, such as "She taught me that I'm unconditionally loved."
You'll be able to appreciate the time you've spent together and feel reenergized about all the fun times ahead by reminding yourself of all the benefits your spouse has brought to your life.

 # SECRET 3

Be of service to your partner

Love is an action-based relationship. Because of this, most individuals attempt to chase romantic and intimate sensations rather than providing for their partner. They don't understand that when you lead with your actions, your emotions will follow. Do you still remember all the sweet things you did for one another when you first started dating? Reconsider that. It doesn't have to be a grand gesture; you might start by assisting them with duties that you are aware make them anxious or by serving their favorite food to them in an unexpected setting or manner. Plan an unexpected surprise for them, like a weekend vacation for the two of you in a nearby city. Your brain would be reminded that your relationship is important to you by doing actions like these.

SECRET 4

Take a Break

Even if it's ironic, it works. When falling in love is the goal, space may revive flames like magic. You may both need to put some distance between you when things start to become a little strange and sticky. Spend a few weeks with a cousin, take a vacation, or even go on a mission; there's no harm in helping others while mending your connection. Give yourself a few days or a week to recall who you are as a person rather than disappearing for a month or a year to do this. When this happens, issues may arise in relationships since neither party has been able to develop outside of their spouse.

SECRET 5

Examine Your Argument Thoroughly

Sometimes, when you find your relationship with your life partner deteriorating, the cause may not be a loss of passion but rather the existence of resentment. When this is the case, it is usually because you perceive yourself as the victim and your spouse as the antagonist. When one partner is unhappy, it is impossible to continue falling in love with your mate. Try sitting down and reflecting in depth for a time rather than allowing things to worsen and wallowing in your resentment. Think about things from your partner's perspective and attempt to understand what they want from you and the relationship; you may be surprised to learn that all your partner needed was some relaxation or a simple embrace.

SECRET 6

Be There

Chances are, whether you're married, cohabitating, or merely in a committed relationship while living apart, the majority of your time together is taken up with other activities. Your focus may be completely diverted by things like the kids, TV, social media, job (particularly if you work from home), or phone calls. Your relationship may benefit greatly by disconnecting from the hectic world outside of you in order to spend time, be present, and connect with your spouse. Being present helps you realize that you're a team and you selected your spouse, so why stop now? Being present is one of the quickest methods to rekindle emotions with your spouse.

 # SECRET 7

Be foolish together

Having fun together with your spouse is not only enjoyable, but also vital to your relationship. Couples who have fun and laugh together are believed to be happy, preserve their spark, and remain together over the long haul. You must see your partner as a friend since you are partners rather than simply family members. So instead of concentrating only on specific emotions, consider taking a break and having some fun with your partner. Try watching comedies together or stand-up comedy as a starting point if you aren't precisely the comic. Yes, inspiration is needed even for comedy.

SECRET 8

Learn to let things go

We sometimes have a tendency to get a little sensitive. Every time someone takes offense at something little or over thinks something that someone else did, a crisis results. You don't have to respond to every little mistake, so do your hardest to break the habit and make the decision to let things go.
When you see that you're becoming overly angry with your spouse, check yourself. Consider if what they did is a problem, particularly if it will have consequences in the future; if not, flush it. Marriage

problems may sometimes be laughed off in order to help you recognize their triviality.

 # SECRET 9

Be Observant

Going about your hectic daily life makes it simple to lose sight of the importance of the things around you. You spend a lot of time or every day with them, but do you also see the other person? Focus more on their abilities, recent physical appearance, development as a person, and performance at work, school, or parenting. This will serve as a reminder of your attraction to them.

 # SECRET 10

Alternate Surprises

Never undervalue the impact of a surprise; it maintains the level of anticipation at an all-time high. Sometimes all it would take is a surprise lunch or date night to fix your connection. If you're married, hire a nanny for the kids so that you may go away with your spouse for some private time. Take turns organizing your date evenings to increase the enjoyment and share the work. Make it personal, enjoyable, and spontaneous while keeping the other person in the dark about the location and activities involved. Even if the date wasn't exactly what you had in mind, you both need to be open to one another's suggestions and try to make the most of it.

You might both be a little selfish and share something you enjoy with the other person if you took turns doing this. This is one of the main strategies to spice up your romantic relationships and develop deeper degrees of closeness.

SECRET 11

Think back

There's a reason why individuals save their family and wedding photo albums; these keepsakes allow us to relive our most memorable occasions. Whether you do it by yourself or with your lover, it wouldn't hurt to take a trip down memory lane. Keep in mind the enjoyable trips you made together, the uncomfortable and spicier moments, and even the challenging periods you overcame as a couple.

Remember that this individual is still the same one you fell in love with and that they probably still have the same amazing personality. You'd feel more connected to your lover if you concentrated more on it.

SECRET 12

Eliminate clutter

Not only can decluttering improve the appearance of your house, but it may also improve the cleanliness of your marriage. You may wonder, "What would you be getting rid of?" The little grudges you harbored from the past include casual remarks made in a fit of rage, negligence, resentment against your partner over something they may not even be aware of, or even a present unresolved conflict. Such activities are necessary for helping couples rediscover their first feelings of love. Don't let them clutter up your thoughts; instead, push them out of there. Decluttering is dealing with issues and, as a result, seeking solutions to make them a thing of the past rather than repressing or ignoring them. The best way to do this is for you and your spouse to have thorough conversations, working through even the challenging issues so you can leave them behind you and enjoy a wonderful time.

SECRET 13

Add Some Flavor in the Bedroom

Any relationship has to be intimate; if there is a problem, it may have repercussions and may be the cause of your feeling distanced from one another. You should definitely sit down and have a conversation with your spouse to assist them appreciate the importance of good intimacy if they have been avoiding it or have possibly forgotten to enjoy it as much as they once did. That bond between spouses has a significant role in establishing their unity and maintaining love.

On the other side, you need to step up and take action if you are the one who is purposefully or unintentionally disregarding or neglecting your partner's needs. Change things up and try something fresh if intimacy has become monotonous. To maintain your physical connection, remember to ask for what you want or need.

#SECRET 14

Demonstrate Your Feelings

It's important for couples to realize early on that showing love doesn't necessarily have to be sexual. There are several methods to demonstrate your relationship status. Of course, a little physical contact here and there during the day will work. You shouldn't be at a loss for words when it comes to showing your partner your love just because you see each other every day. Don't restrict your kissing to the morning before you go for work or the evening after you both return from work. Keep the love alive by giving each other frequent pecks or kisses throughout the day. You may also play goofy games, make jokes, share tales, and be friends.

SECRET 15

Take Action

Falling in love again with your partner requires you to take action. The power of action cannot be underestimated if you desire to rekindle long lasting love in your relationship.

Take a chance and devise action points that bring back all the love you have always desired.

CHAPTER FOUR

THE BIG QUESTIONS???

Can you fall in love again?

Yes, even when things in your relationship appear to have taken a horrible turn, you can fall in love again. The resolve of both parties is all that is necessary. Rekindling your love for your lover will need a substantial amount of effort and dedication, just like everything worthwhile in life.

How can I make my spouse and I fall in love once more?

Don't wait to experience the emotions; start by treating them with respect, care, and love. Fake it 'til you make it. Be thoughtful and, for a change, consider what your partner wants and what's best for them before acting in a way that just benefits you. Stop concentrating on what your partner is doing incorrectly and try to concentrate more on what they are doing well.

If you genuinely loved someone, can you ever stop loving them?

it's possible for the sentiments of love to wane with time. Even those between individuals who really and profoundly love each other need effort if they are to last. However, real love that was founded on honesty and trust is simple to reignite.

In conclusion, keep in mind that lasting love requires more than just a sensation. Put your best effort forward to give your relationship a fighting shot.

www.ingramcontent.com/pod-product-compliance
Lightning Source LLC
LaVergne TN
LVHW052109160826
845678LV00015B/3449
9798846450011